# 5-Ingredient Vegan

## Minimalist Plant-Based Cooking For Beginners

Macy Schumer

Copyright © 2024 by Macy Schumer.

All rights reserved. No part of this publication may be reproduced, distributed, or transmitted in any form, including recording, photocopying, or other electronic or mechanical methods, without the prior written permission of the publisher, except in the case of brief quotations embodied in critical reviews and certain other non-commercial uses per- mitted by copyright law.

Printed in the United States of America

# Introduction

# Why 5-Ingredient Vegan Cooking?

Welcome to *5-Ingredient Vegan: Minimalist Plant-Based Cooking for Beginners*! If you've ever felt overwhelmed by long ingredient lists, complex recipes, or the misconception that vegan cooking is expensive or time-consuming, you're in the right place. This cookbook is designed to make plant-based eating as simple, accessible, and delicious as possible. With just five ingredients (plus pantry staples), you'll be able to create wholesome, satisfying meals that nourish your body and delight your taste buds.

The beauty of 5-ingredient cooking lies in its simplicity. Minimal ingredients mean less prep time, fewer trips to the grocery store, and a streamlined approach to making food. Whether you're new to veganism, a busy professional, or just someone who appreciates fuss-free meals, this book will be your guide to effortless plant-based eating.

## The Power of Plant-Based Eating

Adopting a plant-based diet has numerous benefits, from improved health to a lighter environmental footprint. Studies have shown that plant-based diets can help reduce the risk of chronic diseases like heart disease, diabetes, and certain cancers. They also promote better digestion, clearer skin, and increased energy levels.

Beyond personal health, eating plant-based contributes to sustainability. Animal agriculture is a leading contributor to greenhouse gas emissions, deforestation, and water pollution. By embracing more plant-based meals, you are making a positive impact on the planet while enjoying vibrant, flavorful food.

## Making Vegan Cooking Easy and Accessible

One of the biggest myths about vegan cooking is that it requires exotic ingredients or complicated techniques. The truth is, delicious plant-based meals can be made from simple, everyday ingredients found in most grocery stores. This cookbook emphasizes using whole, unprocessed foods to create balanced meals with minimal effort.

Each recipe in this book includes just five main ingredients, carefully selected to ensure maximum flavor and nutrition. These meals are designed to be beginner-friendly, requiring little cooking experience and minimal kitchen equipment. Whether you're whipping up a hearty breakfast, a quick lunch, or a satisfying dinner, you'll find that plant-based cooking can be as easy as it is delicious.

## What You'll Find in This Cookbook

This book is more than just a collection of recipes; it's a roadmap to a simpler, healthier way of eating. Inside, you'll discover:

- **Quick and Easy Recipes:** Every dish uses just five key ingredients, making meal prep a breeze.
- **Budget-Friendly Meals:** Eating vegan doesn't have to be expensive. These recipes prioritize affordable, everyday ingredients.
- **Nutritious and Balanced Dishes:** Despite the simplicity, each recipe is designed to provide essential nutrients, including protein, fiber, and healthy fats.
- **Time-Saving Tips:** Learn how to stock your pantry with versatile staples, plan meals efficiently, and make the most of your ingredients.

## How to Use This Book

To make your cooking experience as smooth as possible, here are a few guidelines:

1. **Pantry Staples** – While each recipe lists only five main ingredients, a few basic staples (like olive oil, salt, and spices) are assumed to be in your kitchen.
2. **Ingredient Swaps** – If you don't have a specific ingredient on hand, look for substitution tips provided throughout the book.
3. **Meal Planning** – Use the recipes as inspiration for creating a weekly meal plan with minimal shopping and preparation.
4. **Cooking Techniques** – The recipes are designed to be simple, but helpful tips on cooking methods and techniques are included to enhance your skills.

### Embrace the Simplicity

Minimalist cooking isn't just about convenience; it's about embracing the beauty of simple, wholesome ingredients. When you strip down a dish to its essential components, the natural flavors shine through. You'll find that with the right combination of ingredients, even the simplest meals can be incredibly satisfying.

By the end of this book, you'll have the confidence to prepare a variety of plant-based meals without stress or hassle. Whether you're making a creamy avocado pasta, a hearty lentil soup, or a refreshing fruit smoothie, you'll see that less truly can be more in the kitchen.

So, grab your ingredients, get ready to simplify your meals, and let's start cooking!

# Contents

Introduction ..................................................................................................................5
## Why 5-Ingredient Vegan Cooking? ....................................................................5
### What You'll Find in This Cookbook ................................................................5
### How to Use This Book ....................................................................................6
5-Ingredient Vegan Recipes ......................................................................................11
## BREAKFAST RECIPES ..........................................................................................11
    1. Banana Oat Pancakes ................................................................................12
    2. Avocado Toast ............................................................................................13
    3. Chia Pudding ..............................................................................................14
    4. Peanut Butter Banana Smoothie ..............................................................15
    5. Coconut Yogurt with Granola ...................................................................16
    6. Berry Smoothie Bowl .................................................................................17
    7. Almond Butter Toast ..................................................................................18
    8. Mango Coconut Parfait ..............................................................................19
    9. Chocolate Banana Smoothie .....................................................................20
    10. Cinnamon Apple Oatmeal .......................................................................21
    11. Peanut Butter Apple Slices ......................................................................22
    12. Coconut Banana Bites .............................................................................23
    13. Blueberry Almond Butter Toast ...............................................................24
    14. Strawberry Chia Pudding .........................................................................25
    15. Cashew Butter Banana Wrap ..................................................................26
    16. Vanilla Coconut Smoothie .......................................................................27
    17. Chocolate Chia Seed Pudding .................................................................28
    18. Almond Milk Overnight Oats ....................................................................29
    19. Maple Walnut Granola Bars .....................................................................30
    20. Sesame Date Energy Balls ......................................................................31
    21. Cinnamon Apple Oatmeal .......................................................................32
    22. Peanut Butter Granola Bowl ....................................................................33
    23. Raspberry Coconut Smoothie .................................................................34
    24. Mango Chia Pudding ...............................................................................35
    25. Chocolate Almond Butter Toast ...............................................................36

26. Cashew Date Smoothie ........................................................................... 37
27. Avocado Banana Mash on Toast ........................................................... 38
28. Apple Peanut Butter Slices .................................................................... 39
29. Coconut Date Energy Bites ................................................................... 40
30. Banana Walnut Overnight Oats ............................................................ 41

## LUNCH RECIPES .......................................................................................... 42

1. Chickpea Avocado Salad Wrap ............................................................. 43
2. Quinoa & Black Bean Bowl ................................................................... 44
3. Hummus & Cucumber Sandwich .......................................................... 45
4. Lentil & Spinach Soup ........................................................................... 46
5. Sweet Potato & Black Bean Tacos ........................................................ 47
6. Tomato Basil Pasta ................................................................................ 48
7. Chickpea Salad Bowl ............................................................................. 49
8. Avocado Chickpea Toast ....................................................................... 50
9. Vegan Lentil Wrap ................................................................................. 51
10. Mediterranean Quinoa Salad ................................................................ 52
11. Spinach & Mushroom Stir-Fry .............................................................. 53
12. Vegan Pesto Zoodles ............................................................................. 54
13. Roasted Chickpea Wrap ........................................................................ 55
14. Vegan Cucumber Sushi Rolls ................................................................ 56
15. Spicy Peanut Noodles ........................................................................... 57
16. Hummus & Veggie Wrap ...................................................................... 58
17. Black Bean Avocado Bowl .................................................................... 59
18. Sweet Potato & Black Bean Tacos ........................................................ 60
19. Easy Chickpea Salad ............................................................................. 61
20. Peanut Butter Banana Roll-Up .............................................................. 62
21. Quinoa & Avocado Bowl ...................................................................... 63
22. Spinach & Hummus Wrap ..................................................................... 64
23. Lentil & Tomato Salad .......................................................................... 65
24. Vegan Pesto Pasta ................................................................................. 66
25. Chickpea & Avocado Toast .................................................................. 67
26. Avocado & Cucumber Sushi Rolls ....................................................... 68
27. Tomato Basil Toast ............................................................................... 69

- 28. Spicy Lentil Wrap ..................................................................................... 70
- 29. Cucumber & Avocado Salad ................................................................... 71
- 30. Roasted Chickpea Wrap .......................................................................... 72

## DINNER RECIPES ............................................................................................ 73

- 1. Garlic Mushroom Quinoa ......................................................................... 74
- 2. Lentil Tomato Stew ................................................................................... 75
- 3. Chickpea Stir-Fry ...................................................................................... 76
- 4. Sweet Potato & Black Bean Tacos ........................................................... 77
- 5. Avocado Pasta .......................................................................................... 78
- 6. Teriyaki Tofu Bowl .................................................................................... 79
- 7. Quinoa & Roasted Veggie Bowl ............................................................... 80
- 8. Spaghetti Marinara ................................................................................... 81
- 9. Black Bean & Rice Bowl ........................................................................... 82
- 10. Stuffed Bell Peppers ............................................................................... 83
- 11. Garlic Spinach Rice ................................................................................. 84
- 12. Cauliflower Chickpea Curry .................................................................... 85
- 13. Avocado Chickpea Salad ........................................................................ 86
- 14. Roasted Sweet Potato & Kale ................................................................. 87
- 15. Zucchini Noodles with Pesto .................................................................. 88
- 16. Vegan Chili ............................................................................................... 89
- 17. Roasted Brussels Sprouts & Quinoa ..................................................... 90
- 18. Tofu & Spinach Stir-Fry ........................................................................... 91
- 19. Roasted Carrot & Lentil Bowl ................................................................. 92
- 20. Garlic Roasted Cauliflower & Lentils .................................................... 93
- 21. Black Bean Tacos .................................................................................... 94
- 22. Sweet Potato & Black Bean Bowl ........................................................... 95
- 23. Chickpea & Spinach Wrap ...................................................................... 96
- 24. Tomato & Basil Pasta .............................................................................. 97
- 25. Lentil & Tomato Soup .............................................................................. 98
- 26. Roasted Broccoli & Quinoa Bowl ........................................................... 99
- 27. Sautéed Mushrooms & Brown Rice ....................................................... 100
- 28. Spicy Peanut Noodles ............................................................................. 101
- 29. Roasted Chickpeas & Veggies ................................................................ 102

30. Quinoa & Avocado Bowl ................................................................. 103

**SNACK RECIPES** ............................................................................... 104

   1. Almond Butter Apple Slices ........................................................ 106

   2. Avocado Rice Cakes .................................................................... 107

   3. Banana Peanut Butter Bites ....................................................... 108

   4. Hummus & Cucumber Bites ...................................................... 109

   5. Roasted Chickpeas ..................................................................... 110

   6. Dark Chocolate Almond Clusters .............................................. 111

   7. Peanut Butter Oat Balls ............................................................. 112

   8. Stuffed Dates .............................................................................. 113

   9. Veggie Wraps ............................................................................. 114

   10. Baked Sweet Potato Chips ...................................................... 115

   11. Cucumber & Hummus Roll-Ups ............................................. 116

   12. Coconut Date Energy Bites ..................................................... 117

   13. Chocolate-Dipped Strawberries .............................................. 118

   14. Guacamole & Crackers ............................................................ 119

   15. Roasted Chickpeas ................................................................... 120

**ENJOY YOUR MEALS** ....................................................................... 121

5-Ingredient Vegan Recipes

# BREAKFAST RECIPES

## 1. Banana Oat Pancakes

**Prep Time:** 5 minutes
**Cook Time:** 10 minutes
**Servings:** 2

**Ingredients:**

- 1 cup rolled oats
- 1 large ripe banana
- 1 cup almond milk
- 1 teaspoon baking powder
- 1 teaspoon vanilla extract

**Instructions:**

1. Blend all ingredients in a blender until smooth.
2. Heat a non-stick pan over medium heat and pour in small amounts of batter.
3. Cook for about 2 minutes on one side, then flip and cook for another 1-2 minutes.
4. Serve warm with fruit or maple syrup.

**Nutritional Information (Per Serving):**

- Cal: 250 kcal
- Fat: 5 g
- Carbs: 45 g
- Protein: 6 g
- Fiber: 6 g

**Common Allergens:** Nuts (almond milk), Gluten (if using non-certified gluten-free oats)

## 2. Avocado Toast

**Prep Time:** 5 minutes
**Cook Time:** 0 minutes
**Servings:** 2

**Ingredients:**

- 2 slices whole-grain bread
- 1 ripe avocado
- 1 teaspoon lemon juice
- 1 pinch salt
- 1 pinch black pepper

**Instructions:**

1. Toast the bread until golden brown.
2. Mash the avocado with lemon juice, salt, and pepper.
3. Spread onto toasted bread and serve immediately.

**Nutritional Information (Per Serving):**

- Cal: 280 kcal
- Fat: 14 g
- Carbs: 34 g
- Protein: 6 g
- Fiber: 8 g

**Common Allergens:** Gluten (bread)

### 3. Chia Pudding

**Prep Time:** 5 minutes
**Cook Time:** 0 minutes (overnight soak)
**Servings:** 2

**Ingredients:**

- 4 tablespoons chia seeds
- 1 cup coconut milk
- 1 tablespoon maple syrup
- 1 teaspoon vanilla extract
- 1/2 cup fresh berries

**Instructions:**

1. Mix chia seeds, coconut milk, maple syrup, and vanilla extract in a bowl.
2. Stir well and let sit for 5 minutes, then stir again to prevent clumping.
3. Cover and refrigerate overnight.
4. Top with fresh berries before serving.

**Nutritional Information (Per Serving):**

- Cal: 300 kcal
- Fat: 20 g
- Carbs: 30 g
- Protein: 5 g
- Fiber: 10 g

**Common Allergens:** None

## 4. Peanut Butter Banana Smoothie

**Prep Time:** 5 minutes
**Cook Time:** 0 minutes
**Servings:** 2

**Ingredients:**

- 2 bananas
- 2 tablespoons peanut butter
- 1 cup almond milk
- 1 teaspoon cinnamon
- 1 teaspoon maple syrup

**Instructions:**

1. Blend all ingredients until smooth.
2. Pour into glasses and serve immediately.

**Nutritional Information (Per Serving):**

- Cal: 320 kcal
- Fat: 12 g
- Carbs: 45 g
- Protein: 8 g
- Fiber: 6 g

**Common Allergens:** Nuts (peanut butter, almond milk)

## 5. Coconut Yogurt with Granola

**Prep Time:** 5 minutes
**Cook Time:** 0 minutes
**Servings:** 2

**Ingredients:**

- 1 cup coconut yogurt
- 1/2 cup granola
- 1/2 cup fresh berries
- 1 tablespoon maple syrup
- 1 teaspoon shredded coconut

**Instructions:**

1. Divide the coconut yogurt into two bowls.
2. Top with granola, berries, maple syrup, and shredded coconut.
3. Serve immediately.

**Nutritional Information (Per Serving):**

- Cal: 280 kcal
- Fat: 12 g
- Carbs: 40 g
- Protein: 5 g
- Fiber: 6 g

**Common Allergens:** Nuts (granola may contain nuts), Gluten (granola may contain gluten)

## 6. Berry Smoothie Bowl

**Prep Time:** 5 minutes
**Cook Time:** 0 minutes
**Servings:** 2

**Ingredients:**

- 1 cup frozen mixed berries
- 1 frozen banana
- 1/2 cup almond milk
- 1 tablespoon chia seeds
- 1 tablespoon granola

**Instructions:**

1. Blend frozen berries, banana, and almond milk until smooth.
2. Pour into a bowl and top with chia seeds and granola.
3. Serve immediately.

**Nutritional Information (Per Serving):**

- Cal: 220 kcal
- Fat: 6 g
- Carbs: 40 g
- Protein: 5 g
- Fiber: 8 g

**Common Allergens:** Nuts (almond milk), Gluten (granola may contain gluten)

## 7. Almond Butter Toast

**Prep Time:** 5 minutes
**Cook Time:** 0 minutes
**Servings:** 2

**Ingredients:**

- 2 slices whole-grain bread
- 2 tablespoons almond butter
- 1 banana (sliced)
- 1 teaspoon maple syrup
- 1 teaspoon chia seeds

**Instructions:**

1. Toast the bread.
2. Spread almond butter on each slice.
3. Top with banana slices, drizzle with maple syrup, and sprinkle chia seeds.
4. Serve immediately.

**Nutritional Information (Per Serving):**

- Cal: 310 kcal
- Fat: 14 g
- Carbs: 38 g
- Protein: 7 g
- Fiber: 6 g

**Common Allergens:** Nuts (almond butter), Gluten (bread)

## 8. Mango Coconut Parfait

**Prep Time:** 5 minutes
**Cook Time:** 0 minutes
**Servings:** 2

**Ingredients:**

- 1 cup coconut yogurt
- 1/2 cup diced mango
- 1/4 cup granola
- 1 tablespoon shredded coconut
- 1 teaspoon maple syrup

**Instructions:**

1. Layer coconut yogurt and mango in a glass.
2. Top with granola, shredded coconut, and maple syrup.
3. Serve immediately.

**Nutritional Information (Per Serving):**

- Cal: 290 kcal
- Fat: 12 g
- Carbs: 39 g
- Protein: 4 g
- Fiber: 5 g

**Common Allergens:** Nuts (granola may contain nuts), Gluten (granola may contain gluten)

## 9. Chocolate Banana Smoothie

**Prep Time:** 5 minutes
**Cook Time:** 0 minutes
**Servings:** 2

**Ingredients:**

- 2 bananas
- 1 cup almond milk
- 1 tablespoon cocoa powder
- 1 teaspoon vanilla extract
- 1 tablespoon maple syrup

**Instructions:**

1. Blend all ingredients until smooth.
2. Pour into glasses and serve immediately.

**Nutritional Information (Per Serving):**

- Cal: 250 kcal
- Fat: 4 g
- Carbs: 50 g
- Protein: 5 g
- Fiber: 6 g

**Common Allergens:** Nuts (almond milk)

## 10. Cinnamon Apple Oatmeal

**Prep Time:** 5 minutes
**Cook Time:** 5 minutes
**Servings:** 2

**Ingredients:**

- 1 cup rolled oats
- 1 apple (diced)
- 1 teaspoon cinnamon
- 1 cup almond milk
- 1 tablespoon maple syrup

**Instructions:**

1. Cook oats with almond milk over medium heat.
2. Add diced apple and cinnamon, stir well.
3. Once thickened, drizzle with maple syrup and serve.

**Nutritional Information (Per Serving):**

- Cal: 270 kcal
- Fat: 5 g
- Carbs: 50 g
- Protein: 7 g
- Fiber: 7 g

**Common Allergens:** Nuts (almond milk), Gluten (if using non-certified gluten-free oats)

## 11. Peanut Butter Apple Slices

**Prep Time:** 5 minutes
**Cook Time:** 0 minutes
**Servings:** 2

**Ingredients:**

- 1 apple (sliced)
- 2 tablespoons peanut butter
- 1 teaspoon cinnamon
- 1 tablespoon granola
- 1 teaspoon maple syrup

**Instructions:**

1. Spread peanut butter on each apple slice.
2. Sprinkle with cinnamon, granola, and drizzle with maple syrup.
3. Serve immediately.

**Nutritional Information (Per Serving):**

- Cal: 280 kcal
- Fat: 12 g
- Carbs: 35 g
- Protein: 6 g
- Fiber: 6 g

**Common Allergens:** Nuts (peanut butter), Gluten (granola may contain gluten)

## 12. Coconut Banana Bites

**Prep Time:** 5 minutes
**Cook Time:** 0 minutes
**Servings:** 2

**Ingredients:**

- 1 banana (sliced)
- 2 tablespoons shredded coconut
- 1 tablespoon almond butter
- 1 teaspoon chia seeds
- 1 teaspoon maple syrup

**Instructions:**

1. Dip banana slices in almond butter.
2. Sprinkle with shredded coconut and chia seeds.
3. Drizzle with maple syrup and serve immediately.

**Nutritional Information (Per Serving):**

- Cal: 250 kcal
- Fat: 10 g
- Carbs: 38 g
- Protein: 5 g
- Fiber: 6 g

**Common Allergens:** Nuts (almond butter)

## 13. Blueberry Almond Butter Toast

**Prep Time:** 5 minutes
**Cook Time:** 0 minutes
**Servings:** 2

**Ingredients:**

- 2 slices whole-grain bread
- 2 tablespoons almond butter
- 1/2 cup fresh blueberries
- 1 teaspoon maple syrup
- 1 teaspoon chia seeds

**Instructions:**

1. Toast the bread until golden brown.
2. Spread almond butter evenly on each slice.
3. Top with fresh blueberries, drizzle with maple syrup, and sprinkle with chia seeds.
4. Serve immediately.

**Nutritional Information (Per Serving):**

- Cal: 320 kcal
- Fat: 14 g
- Carbs: 40 g
- Protein: 7 g
- Fiber: 6 g

**Common Allergens:** Nuts (almond butter), Gluten (bread)

## 14. Strawberry Chia Pudding

**Prep Time:** 5 minutes
**Cook Time:** 0 minutes (overnight soak)
**Servings:** 2

**Ingredients:**

- 1 cup almond milk
- 4 tablespoons chia seeds
- 1/2 cup fresh strawberries (sliced)
- 1 tablespoon maple syrup
- 1 teaspoon vanilla extract

**Instructions:**

1. In a bowl, mix almond milk, chia seeds, maple syrup, and vanilla extract.
2. Stir well, let sit for 5 minutes, then stir again to prevent clumping.
3. Cover and refrigerate overnight.
4. Before serving, top with sliced strawberries.

**Nutritional Information (Per Serving):**

- Cal: 280 kcal
- Fat: 10 g
- Carbs: 38 g
- Protein: 6 g
- Fiber: 8 g

**Common Allergens:** Nuts (almond milk)

## 15. Cashew Butter Banana Wrap

**Prep Time:** 5 minutes
**Cook Time:** 0 minutes
**Servings:** 2

**Ingredients:**

- 2 whole wheat tortillas
- 2 tablespoons cashew butter
- 1 banana (sliced)
- 1 teaspoon cinnamon
- 1 teaspoon maple syrup

**Instructions:**

1. Spread cashew butter evenly over each tortilla.
2. Place banana slices in the center.
3. Sprinkle with cinnamon and drizzle with maple syrup.
4. Roll up tightly, slice in half, and serve.

**Nutritional Information (Per Serving):**

- Cal: 320 kcal
- Fat: 12 g
- Carbs: 42 g
- Protein: 7 g
- Fiber: 6 g

**Common Allergens:** Nuts (cashew butter), Gluten (tortilla)

## 16. Vanilla Coconut Smoothie

**Prep Time:** 5 minutes
**Cook Time:** 0 minutes
**Servings:** 2

**Ingredients:**

- 1 banana
- 1 cup coconut milk
- 1 teaspoon vanilla extract
- 1 tablespoon shredded coconut
- 1 teaspoon maple syrup

**Instructions:**

1. Blend all ingredients until smooth.
2. Pour into glasses and serve immediately.

**Nutritional Information (Per Serving):**

- Cal: 260 kcal
- Fat: 14 g
- Carbs: 35 g
- Protein: 3 g
- Fiber: 5 g

**Common Allergens:** None

## 17. Chocolate Chia Seed Pudding

**Prep Time:** 5 minutes
**Cook Time:** 0 minutes (overnight soak)
**Servings:** 2

**Ingredients:**

- 4 tablespoons chia seeds
- 1 cup almond milk
- 1 tablespoon cocoa powder
- 1 tablespoon maple syrup
- 1 teaspoon vanilla extract

**Instructions:**

1. In a bowl, mix almond milk, chia seeds, cocoa powder, maple syrup, and vanilla extract.
2. Stir well, let sit for 5 minutes, then stir again.
3. Cover and refrigerate overnight.
4. Serve chilled.

**Nutritional Information (Per Serving):**

- Cal: 280 kcal
- Fat: 12 g
- Carbs: 30 g
- Protein: 5 g
- Fiber: 8 g

**Common Allergens:** Nuts (almond milk)

## 18. Almond Milk Overnight Oats

**Prep Time:** 5 minutes
**Cook Time:** 0 minutes (overnight soak)
**Servings:** 2

**Ingredients:**

- 1 cup rolled oats
- 1 cup almond milk
- 1 tablespoon chia seeds
- 1 tablespoon maple syrup
- 1 teaspoon vanilla extract

**Instructions:**

1. Mix oats, almond milk, chia seeds, maple syrup, and vanilla extract in a jar.
2. Stir well, cover, and refrigerate overnight.
3. Serve chilled with optional fruit toppings.

**Nutritional Information (Per Serving):**

- Cal: 270 kcal
- Fat: 7 g
- Carbs: 45 g
- Protein: 7 g
- Fiber: 6 g

**Common Allergens:** Nuts (almond milk), Gluten (if using non-certified gluten-free oats)

## 19. Maple Walnut Granola Bars

**Prep Time:** 10 minutes
**Cook Time:** 0 minutes (refrigerate for 1 hour)
**Servings:** 4

**Ingredients:**

- 1 cup rolled oats
- 1/2 cup walnuts (chopped)
- 1/4 cup almond butter
- 2 tablespoons maple syrup
- 1 teaspoon cinnamon

**Instructions:**

1. Mix all ingredients in a bowl until well combined.
2. Press mixture into a parchment-lined baking dish.
3. Refrigerate for at least 1 hour, then slice into bars.
4. Serve chilled.

**Nutritional Information (Per Serving):**

- Cal: 300 kcal
- Fat: 15 g
- Carbs: 35 g
- Protein: 7 g
- Fiber: 5 g

**Common Allergens:** Nuts (walnuts, almond butter), Gluten (if using non-certified gluten-free oats)

## 20. Sesame Date Energy Balls

**Prep Time:** 10 minutes
**Cook Time:** 0 minutes (chill for 30 minutes)
**Servings:** 6 (Makes 12 small balls)

**Ingredients:**

- 1 cup dates (pitted)
- 1/2 cup almonds
- 1/4 cup sesame seeds
- 1 tablespoon cocoa powder
- 1 teaspoon vanilla extract

**Instructions:**

1. Blend all ingredients in a food processor until sticky dough forms.
2. Roll into small balls and coat with additional sesame seeds if desired.
3. Refrigerate for 30 minutes before serving.

**Nutritional Information (Per Serving):**

- Cal: 180 kcal
- Fat: 8 g
- Carbs: 24 g
- Protein: 4 g
- Fiber: 3 g

**Common Allergens:** Nuts (almonds), Sesame

## 21. Cinnamon Apple Oatmeal

**Prep Time:** 5 minutes
**Cook Time:** 5 minutes
**Servings:** 2

**Ingredients:**

- 1 cup rolled oats
- 1 apple (chopped)
- 1 cup almond milk
- 1 teaspoon cinnamon
- 1 tablespoon maple syrup

**Instructions:**

1. In a pot, heat almond milk over medium heat.
2. Stir in oats and cook for 3-5 minutes, stirring occasionally.
3. Add chopped apple, cinnamon, and maple syrup. Stir well.
4. Serve warm.

**Nutritional Information (Per Serving):**

- Cal: 290 kcal
- Fat: 6 g
- Carbs: 50 g
- Protein: 6 g
- Fiber: 7 g

**Common Allergens:** Nuts (almond milk), Gluten (if using non-certified gluten-free oats)

## 22. Peanut Butter Granola Bowl

**Prep Time:** 5 minutes
**Cook Time:** 0 minutes
**Servings:** 2

**Ingredients:**

- 1 cup granola
- 2 tablespoons peanut butter
- 1 cup coconut yogurt
- 1 tablespoon maple syrup
- 1/2 cup sliced bananas

**Instructions:**

1. Divide coconut yogurt into two bowls.
2. Top with granola, peanut butter, and sliced bananas.
3. Drizzle with maple syrup and serve.

**Nutritional Information (Per Serving):**

- Cal: 350 kcal
- Fat: 15 g
- Carbs: 45 g
- Protein: 8 g
- Fiber: 6 g

**Common Allergens:** Nuts (peanut butter), Gluten (granola may contain gluten)

## 23. Raspberry Coconut Smoothie

**Prep Time:** 5 minutes
**Cook Time:** 0 minutes
**Servings:** 2

**Ingredients:**

- 1 cup frozen raspberries
- 1 banana
- 1 cup coconut milk
- 1 tablespoon shredded coconut
- 1 teaspoon maple syrup

**Instructions:**

1. Blend all ingredients until smooth.
2. Pour into glasses and serve.

**Nutritional Information (Per Serving):**

- Cal: 250 kcal
- Fat: 10 g
- Carbs: 38 g
- Protein: 3 g
- Fiber: 5 g

**Common Allergens:** None

## 24. Mango Chia Pudding

**Prep Time:** 5 minutes
**Cook Time:** 0 minutes (overnight soak)
**Servings:** 2

**Ingredients:**

- 1 cup coconut milk
- 4 tablespoons chia seeds
- 1/2 cup mango (diced)
- 1 tablespoon maple syrup
- 1 teaspoon vanilla extract

**Instructions:**

1. Mix chia seeds, coconut milk, maple syrup, and vanilla extract in a bowl.
2. Stir well, let sit for 5 minutes, then stir again.
3. Cover and refrigerate overnight.
4. Before serving, top with diced mango.

**Nutritional Information (Per Serving):**

- Cal: 290 kcal
- Fat: 12 g
- Carbs: 35 g
- Protein: 5 g
- Fiber: 6 g

**Common Allergens:** None

## 25. Chocolate Almond Butter Toast

**Prep Time:** 5 minutes
**Cook Time:** 0 minutes
**Servings:** 2

**Ingredients:**

- 2 slices whole-grain bread
- 2 tablespoons almond butter
- 1 tablespoon cocoa powder
- 1 tablespoon maple syrup
- 1 teaspoon chia seeds

**Instructions:**

1. Mix almond butter, cocoa powder, and maple syrup until smooth.
2. Spread on toasted bread and sprinkle with chia seeds.
3. Serve immediately.

**Nutritional Information (Per Serving):**

- Cal: 320 kcal
- Fat: 14 g
- Carbs: 42 g
- Protein: 7 g
- Fiber: 5 g

**Common Allergens:** Nuts (almond butter), Gluten (bread)

## 26. Cashew Date Smoothie

**Prep Time:** 5 minutes
**Cook Time:** 0 minutes
**Servings:** 2

**Ingredients:**

- 2 dates (pitted)
- 1 banana
- 1 cup almond milk
- 1 tablespoon cashew butter
- 1 teaspoon vanilla extract

**Instructions:**

1. Blend all ingredients until smooth.
2. Pour into glasses and serve.

**Nutritional Information (Per Serving):**

- Cal: 270 kcal
- Fat: 9 g
- Carbs: 40 g
- Protein: 5 g
- Fiber: 4 g

**Common Allergens:** Nuts (almond milk, cashew butter)

## 27. Avocado Banana Mash on Toast

**Prep Time:** 5 minutes
**Cook Time:** 0 minutes
**Servings:** 2

**Ingredients:**

- 2 slices whole-grain bread
- 1 ripe avocado
- 1 banana
- 1 teaspoon lemon juice
- 1 pinch salt

**Instructions:**

1. Mash avocado and banana together in a bowl.
2. Stir in lemon juice and salt.
3. Spread onto toasted bread and serve.

**Nutritional Information (Per Serving):**

- Cal: 310 kcal
- Fat: 13 g
- Carbs: 42 g
- Protein: 6 g
- Fiber: 7 g

**Common Allergens:** Gluten (bread)

## 28. Apple Peanut Butter Slices

**Prep Time:** 5 minutes
**Cook Time:** 0 minutes
**Servings:** 2

**Ingredients:**

- 1 apple (sliced)
- 2 tablespoons peanut butter
- 1 teaspoon cinnamon
- 1 teaspoon maple syrup
- 1 teaspoon chia seeds

**Instructions:**

1. Spread peanut butter on each apple slice.
2. Sprinkle with cinnamon, maple syrup, and chia seeds.
3. Serve immediately.

**Nutritional Information (Per Serving):**

- Cal: 250 kcal
- Fat: 10 g
- Carbs: 35 g
- Protein: 6 g
- Fiber: 6 g

**Common Allergens:** Nuts (peanut butter)

## 29. Coconut Date Energy Bites

**Prep Time:** 10 minutes
**Cook Time:** 0 minutes (chill for 30 minutes)
**Servings:** 6 (Makes 12 small balls)

**Ingredients:**

- 1 cup dates (pitted)
- 1/2 cup almonds
- 1/4 cup shredded coconut
- 1 teaspoon vanilla extract
- 1 tablespoon coconut oil

**Instructions:**

1. Blend all ingredients in a food processor until sticky dough forms.
2. Roll into small balls and coat with additional shredded coconut if desired.
3. Refrigerate for 30 minutes before serving.

**Nutritional Information (Per Serving):**

- Cal: 180 kcal
- Fat: 9 g
- Carbs: 24 g
- Protein: 4 g
- Fiber: 3 g

**Common Allergens:** Nuts (almonds)

## 30. Banana Walnut Overnight Oats

**Prep Time:** 5 minutes
**Cook Time:** 0 minutes (overnight soak)
**Servings:** 2

**Ingredients:**

- 1 cup rolled oats
- 1 cup almond milk
- 1 banana (mashed)
- 1/4 cup walnuts (chopped)
- 1 tablespoon maple syrup

**Instructions:**

1. Mix all ingredients in a jar.
2. Stir well, cover, and refrigerate overnight.
3. Serve chilled.

**Nutritional Information (Per Serving):**

- Cal: 290 kcal
- Fat: 10 g
- Carbs: 42 g
- Protein: 7 g
- Fiber: 6 g

**Common Allergens:** Nuts (walnuts, almond milk), Gluten (if using non-certified gluten-free oats)

# LUNCH RECIPES

## 1. Chickpea Avocado Salad Wrap

**Prep Time:** 5 minutes
**Cook Time:** 0 minutes
**Servings:** 2

**Ingredients:**

- 1 cup canned chickpeas, drained and rinsed
- 1 ripe avocado
- 1 teaspoon lemon juice
- 2 whole wheat tortillas
- 1/2 cup shredded carrots

**Instructions:**

1. In a bowl, mash the chickpeas and avocado together until combined.
2. Mix in lemon juice and shredded carrots.
3. Divide mixture between the two tortillas and roll them up.
4. Serve immediately.

**Nutritional Information (Per Serving):**

- **Cal:** 320 kcal
- **Fat:** 12 g
- **Carbs:** 45 g
- **Proteins:** 10 g
- **Fiber:** 10 g

**Common Allergens:** Gluten (wheat tortillas)

## 2. Quinoa & Black Bean Bowl

**Prep Time:** 5 minutes
**Cook Time:** 10 minutes
**Servings:** 2

**Ingredients:**

- 1 cup cooked quinoa
- 1/2 cup canned black beans, drained and rinsed
- 1/2 cup diced tomatoes
- 1/2 avocado, diced
- 1 teaspoon lime juice

**Instructions:**

1. In a bowl, mix the cooked quinoa, black beans, and diced tomatoes.
2. Add lime juice and toss to combine.
3. Top with diced avocado and serve immediately.

**Nutritional Information (Per Serving):**

- **Cal:** 290 kcal
- **Fat:** 8 g
- **Carbs:** 44 g
- **Proteins:** 9 g
- **Fiber:** 9 g

**Common Allergens:** None

## 3. Hummus & Cucumber Sandwich

**Prep Time:** 5 minutes
**Cook Time:** 0 minutes
**Servings:** 1

**Ingredients:**

- 2 slices whole grain bread
- 3 tablespoons hummus
- 1/2 cucumber, thinly sliced
- 1 teaspoon lemon juice
- 1/2 teaspoon black pepper

**Instructions:**

1. Spread hummus evenly over both slices of bread.
2. Layer cucumber slices over the hummus.
3. Drizzle with lemon juice and sprinkle black pepper.
4. Assemble the sandwich and serve.

**Nutritional Information (Per Serving):**

- **Cal:** 280 kcal
- **Fat:** 6 g
- **Carbs:** 45 g
- **Proteins:** 10 g
- **Fiber:** 7 g

**Common Allergens:** Gluten (bread), Sesame (hummus)

## 4. Lentil & Spinach Soup

**Prep Time:** 5 minutes
**Cook Time:** 15 minutes
**Servings:** 2

**Ingredients:**

- 1 cup cooked lentils
- 1 cup vegetable broth
- 1/2 cup spinach, chopped
- 1/2 teaspoon cumin
- 1/2 teaspoon black pepper

**Instructions:**

1. In a pot, heat the vegetable broth over medium heat.
2. Add cooked lentils and cumin, stirring well.
3. Add spinach and let simmer for 5 minutes.
4. Serve warm, seasoned with black pepper.

**Nutritional Information (Per Serving):**

- **Cal:** 230 kcal
- **Fat:** 2 g
- **Carbs:** 35 g
- **Proteins:** 12 g
- **Fiber:** 10 g

**Common Allergens:** None

## 5. Sweet Potato & Black Bean Tacos

**Prep Time:** 10 minutes
**Cook Time:** 15 minutes
**Servings:** 2

**Ingredients:**

- 1 medium sweet potato, diced
- 1/2 cup canned black beans, drained
- 1 teaspoon olive oil
- 1 teaspoon taco seasoning
- 4 small corn tortillas

**Instructions:**

1. Heat olive oil in a pan over medium heat.
2. Sauté sweet potato for 10 minutes until soft.
3. Add black beans and taco seasoning, stir for 5 minutes.
4. Divide the mixture into tortillas and serve warm.

**Nutritional Information (Per Serving):**

- **Cal:** 310 kcal
- **Fat:** 6 g
- **Carbs:** 55 g
- **Proteins:** 10 g
- **Fiber:** 11 g

**Common Allergens:** None

## 6. Tomato Basil Pasta

**Prep Time:** 5 minutes
**Cook Time:** 10 minutes
**Servings:** 2

**Ingredients:**

- 2 cups cooked whole wheat pasta
- 1 cup cherry tomatoes, halved
- 1 tablespoon olive oil
- 1/2 teaspoon garlic powder
- 1/4 cup fresh basil, chopped

**Instructions:**

1. Heat olive oil in a pan over medium heat.
2. Add cherry tomatoes and cook for 5 minutes.
3. Toss in cooked pasta and garlic powder, stirring well.
4. Sprinkle with fresh basil and serve warm.

**Nutritional Information (Per Serving):**

- **Cal:** 320 kcal
- **Fat:** 8 g
- **Carbs:** 55 g
- **Proteins:** 10 g
- **Fiber:** 9 g

**Common Allergens:** Gluten (pasta)

## 7. Chickpea Salad Bowl

**Prep Time:** 5 minutes
**Cook Time:** 0 minutes
**Servings:** 2

**Ingredients:**

- 1 cup canned chickpeas, drained
- 1/2 cup diced cucumber
- 1/2 cup cherry tomatoes, halved
- 1 tablespoon lemon juice
- 1/2 teaspoon black pepper

**Instructions:**

1. In a bowl, combine chickpeas, cucumber, and cherry tomatoes.
2. Drizzle with lemon juice and season with black pepper.
3. Toss and serve immediately.

**Nutritional Information (Per Serving):**

- **Cal:** 250 kcal
- **Fat:** 3 g
- **Carbs:** 42 g
- **Proteins:** 9 g
- **Fiber:** 10 g

**Common Allergens:** None

## 8. Avocado Chickpea Toast

**Prep Time:** 5 minutes
**Cook Time:** 0 minutes
**Servings:** 1

**Ingredients:**

- 1 slice whole grain bread
- 1/2 avocado, mashed
- 1/4 cup canned chickpeas, drained
- 1 teaspoon lemon juice
- 1/4 teaspoon black pepper

**Instructions:**

1. Toast the bread to desired crispness.
2. Spread mashed avocado on top.
3. Mash chickpeas lightly and sprinkle over avocado.
4. Drizzle with lemon juice and season with black pepper.
5. Serve immediately.

**Nutritional Information (Per Serving):**

- **Cal:** 290 kcal
- **Fat:** 11 g
- **Carbs:** 40 g
- **Proteins:** 8 g
- **Fiber:** 9 g

**Common Allergens:** Gluten (bread)

## 9. Vegan Lentil Wrap

**Prep Time:** 10 minutes
**Cook Time:** 5 minutes
**Servings:** 2

**Ingredients:**

- 1 cup cooked lentils
- 1/2 cup shredded carrots
- 1 tablespoon hummus
- 1 teaspoon lemon juice
- 2 whole wheat tortillas

**Instructions:**

1. In a bowl, mix lentils, shredded carrots, hummus, and lemon juice.
2. Spread the mixture evenly onto the tortillas.
3. Roll up the tortillas tightly and serve.

**Nutritional Information (Per Serving):**

- **Cal:** 310 kcal
- **Fat:** 5 g
- **Carbs:** 50 g
- **Proteins:** 12 g
- **Fiber:** 11 g

**Common Allergens:** Gluten (tortillas), Sesame (hummus)

## 10. Mediterranean Quinoa Salad

**Prep Time:** 5 minutes
**Cook Time:** 0 minutes
**Servings:** 2

**Ingredients:**

- 1 cup cooked quinoa
- 1/2 cup cherry tomatoes, halved
- 1/4 cup cucumber, diced
- 1 teaspoon olive oil
- 1 teaspoon lemon juice

**Instructions:**

1. In a bowl, combine cooked quinoa, cherry tomatoes, and cucumber.
2. Drizzle with olive oil and lemon juice.
3. Toss and serve.

**Nutritional Information (Per Serving):**

- **Cal:** 280 kcal
- **Fat:** 7 g
- **Carbs:** 45 g
- **Proteins:** 8 g
- **Fiber:** 6 g

**Common Allergens:** None

## 11. Spinach & Mushroom Stir-Fry

**Prep Time:** 5 minutes
**Cook Time:** 10 minutes
**Servings:** 2

**Ingredients:**

- 1 cup mushrooms, sliced
- 2 cups spinach
- 1 teaspoon olive oil
- 1 teaspoon soy sauce
- 1/2 teaspoon garlic powder

**Instructions:**

1. Heat olive oil in a pan over medium heat.
2. Add mushrooms and cook for 5 minutes until tender.
3. Add spinach and cook for another 3 minutes.
4. Stir in soy sauce and garlic powder.
5. Serve warm.

**Nutritional Information (Per Serving):**

- **Cal:** 150 kcal
- **Fat:** 6 g
- **Carbs:** 18 g
- **Proteins:** 6 g
- **Fiber:** 5 g

**Common Allergens:** Soy (soy sauce)

## 12. Vegan Pesto Zoodles

**Prep Time:** 5 minutes
**Cook Time:** 5 minutes
**Servings:** 2

**Ingredients:**

- 2 zucchini, spiralized
- 2 tablespoons vegan pesto
- 1/4 cup cherry tomatoes, halved
- 1 teaspoon olive oil
- 1/4 teaspoon black pepper

**Instructions:**

1. Heat olive oil in a pan over medium heat.
2. Add spiralized zucchini and cook for 3 minutes.
3. Toss in vegan pesto and cherry tomatoes.
4. Cook for another 2 minutes and season with black pepper.
5. Serve warm.

**Nutritional Information (Per Serving):**

- **Cal:** 180 kcal
- **Fat:** 9 g
- **Carbs:** 22 g
- **Proteins:** 5 g
- **Fiber:** 6 g

**Common Allergens:** Nuts (if pesto contains nuts)

## 13. Roasted Chickpea Wrap

**Prep Time:** 5 minutes
**Cook Time:** 10 minutes
**Servings:** 2

**Ingredients:**

- 1 cup canned chickpeas, drained
- 1 teaspoon olive oil
- 1 teaspoon paprika
- 2 whole wheat tortillas
- 1/2 cup shredded lettuce

**Instructions:**

1. Preheat oven to 375°F (190°C).
2. Toss chickpeas with olive oil and paprika, then roast for 10 minutes.
3. Spread roasted chickpeas onto tortillas.
4. Add shredded lettuce, roll up, and serve.

**Nutritional Information (Per Serving):**

- **Cal:** 300 kcal
- **Fat:** 6 g
- **Carbs:** 50 g
- **Proteins:** 10 g
- **Fiber:** 9 g

**Common Allergens:** Gluten (tortillas)

## 14. Vegan Cucumber Sushi Rolls

**Prep Time:** 10 minutes
**Cook Time:** 0 minutes
**Servings:** 2

**Ingredients:**

- 1 cup cooked sushi rice
- 2 sheets nori seaweed
- 1/2 cucumber, thinly sliced
- 1 teaspoon rice vinegar
- 1 teaspoon sesame seeds

**Instructions:**

1. Spread a thin layer of sushi rice over nori sheets.
2. Arrange cucumber slices on top.
3. Drizzle rice vinegar and roll tightly.
4. Slice into bite-sized pieces and sprinkle with sesame seeds.

**Nutritional Information (Per Serving):**

- **Cal:** 250 kcal
- **Fat:** 2 g
- **Carbs:** 50 g
- **Proteins:** 6 g
- **Fiber:** 5 g

**Common Allergens:** Sesame (sesame seeds)

## 15. Spicy Peanut Noodles

**Prep Time:** 5 minutes
**Cook Time:** 10 minutes
**Servings:** 2

**Ingredients:**

- 2 cups cooked rice noodles
- 1 tablespoon peanut butter
- 1 teaspoon soy sauce
- 1/2 teaspoon chili flakes
- 1/4 cup chopped green onions

**Instructions:**

1. In a bowl, mix peanut butter, soy sauce, and chili flakes.
2. Toss in cooked rice noodles and mix well.
3. Garnish with green onions and serve warm.

**Nutritional Information (Per Serving):**

- **Cal:** 320 kcal
- **Fat:** 8 g
- **Carbs:** 50 g
- **Proteins:** 10 g
- **Fiber:** 5 g

**Common Allergens:** Nuts (peanut butter), Soy (soy sauce)

## 16. Hummus & Veggie Wrap

**Prep Time:** 5 minutes
**Cook Time:** 0 minutes
**Servings:** 2

**Ingredients:**

- 2 whole wheat tortillas
- 1/2 cup hummus
- 1/2 cup shredded carrots
- 1/2 cucumber, sliced
- 1/4 teaspoon black pepper

**Instructions:**

1. Spread hummus evenly on each tortilla.
2. Add shredded carrots and cucumber slices.
3. Sprinkle with black pepper.
4. Roll up the tortillas and serve.

**Nutritional Information (Per Serving):**

- **Cal:** 290 kcal
- **Fat:** 9 g
- **Carbs:** 45 g
- **Proteins:** 9 g
- **Fiber:** 7 g

**Common Allergens:** Gluten (tortillas), Sesame (hummus)

## 17. Black Bean Avocado Bowl

**Prep Time:** 5 minutes
**Cook Time:** 0 minutes
**Servings:** 2

**Ingredients:**

- 1 cup canned black beans, drained
- 1/2 avocado, diced
- 1/2 cup cherry tomatoes, halved
- 1 teaspoon lime juice
- 1/4 teaspoon cumin

**Instructions:**

1. In a bowl, combine black beans, avocado, and cherry tomatoes.
2. Drizzle with lime juice and sprinkle with cumin.
3. Toss gently and serve.

**Nutritional Information (Per Serving):**

- **Cal:** 260 kcal
- **Fat:** 9 g
- **Carbs:** 35 g
- **Proteins:** 10 g
- **Fiber:** 10 g

**Common Allergens:** None

## 18. Sweet Potato & Black Bean Tacos

**Prep Time:** 10 minutes
**Cook Time:** 15 minutes
**Servings:** 2

**Ingredients:**

- 1 small sweet potato, diced
- 1/2 cup canned black beans, drained
- 1 teaspoon olive oil
- 2 small corn tortillas
- 1/2 teaspoon smoked paprika

**Instructions:**

1. Preheat oven to 400°F (200°C).
2. Toss sweet potato with olive oil and smoked paprika, then roast for 15 minutes.
3. Warm the tortillas and fill them with roasted sweet potatoes and black beans.
4. Serve warm.

**Nutritional Information (Per Serving):**

- **Cal:** 300 kcal
- **Fat:** 6 g
- **Carbs:** 55 g
- **Proteins:** 9 g
- **Fiber:** 8 g

**Common Allergens:** None

## 19. Easy Chickpea Salad

**Prep Time:** 5 minutes
**Cook Time:** 0 minutes
**Servings:** 2

**Ingredients:**

- 1 cup canned chickpeas, drained
- 1/2 cucumber, diced
- 1/4 cup red onion, diced
- 1 teaspoon olive oil
- 1 teaspoon lemon juice

**Instructions:**

1. In a bowl, mix chickpeas, cucumber, and red onion.
2. Drizzle with olive oil and lemon juice.
3. Toss and serve.

**Nutritional Information (Per Serving):**

- **Cal:** 240 kcal
- **Fat:** 6 g
- **Carbs:** 35 g
- **Proteins:** 9 g
- **Fiber:** 7 g

**Common Allergens:** None

## 20. Peanut Butter Banana Roll-Up

**Prep Time:** 5 minutes
**Cook Time:** 0 minutes
**Servings:** 1

**Ingredients:**

- 1 whole wheat tortilla
- 1 tablespoon peanut butter
- 1 banana, sliced
- 1 teaspoon maple syrup
- 1/4 teaspoon cinnamon

**Instructions:**

1. Spread peanut butter over the tortilla.
2. Arrange banana slices evenly.
3. Drizzle with maple syrup and sprinkle with cinnamon.
4. Roll up and slice into bite-sized pieces.

**Nutritional Information (Per Serving):**

- **Cal:** 320 kcal
- **Fat:** 10 g
- **Carbs:** 50 g
- **Proteins:** 8 g
- **Fiber:** 6 g

**Common Allergens:** Gluten (tortilla), Nuts (peanut butter)

## 21. Quinoa & Avocado Bowl

**Prep Time:** 5 minutes
**Cook Time:** 12 minutes
**Servings:** 2

**Ingredients:**

- 1 cup cooked quinoa
- 1/2 avocado, diced
- 1/2 cup cherry tomatoes, halved
- 1 teaspoon olive oil
- 1 teaspoon lemon juice

**Instructions:**

1. In a bowl, combine quinoa, avocado, and cherry tomatoes.
2. Drizzle with olive oil and lemon juice.
3. Toss gently and serve.

**Nutritional Information (Per Serving):**

- **Cal:** 280 kcal
- **Fat:** 10 g
- **Carbs:** 40 g
- **Proteins:** 8 g
- **Fiber:** 6 g

**Common Allergens:** None

## 22. Spinach & Hummus Wrap

**Prep Time:** 5 minutes
**Cook Time:** 0 minutes
**Servings:** 2

**Ingredients:**

- 2 whole wheat tortillas
- 1/2 cup hummus
- 1/2 cup baby spinach
- 1/2 cucumber, sliced
- 1/4 teaspoon black pepper

**Instructions:**

1. Spread hummus on each tortilla.
2. Add spinach and cucumber slices.
3. Sprinkle with black pepper.
4. Roll up and serve.

**Nutritional Information (Per Serving):**

- **Cal:** 270 kcal
- **Fat:** 8 g
- **Carbs:** 42 g
- **Proteins:** 9 g
- **Fiber:** 6 g

**Common Allergens:** Gluten (tortillas), Sesame (hummus)

## 23. Lentil & Tomato Salad

**Prep Time:** 5 minutes
**Cook Time:** 0 minutes
**Servings:** 2

**Ingredients:**

- 1 cup cooked lentils
- 1/2 cup cherry tomatoes, halved
- 1/4 cup red onion, diced
- 1 teaspoon olive oil
- 1 teaspoon balsamic vinegar

**Instructions:**

1. In a bowl, combine lentils, cherry tomatoes, and red onion.
2. Drizzle with olive oil and balsamic vinegar.
3. Toss and serve.

**Nutritional Information (Per Serving):**

- **Cal:** 250 kcal
- **Fat:** 6 g
- **Carbs:** 35 g
- **Proteins:** 12 g
- **Fiber:** 8 g

**Common Allergens:** None

## 24. Vegan Pesto Pasta

**Prep Time:** 5 minutes
**Cook Time:** 10 minutes
**Servings:** 2

**Ingredients:**

- 2 cups cooked pasta
- 1/4 cup vegan pesto
- 1/2 cup cherry tomatoes, halved
- 1 teaspoon olive oil
- 1/4 teaspoon black pepper

**Instructions:**

1. Toss cooked pasta with vegan pesto.
2. Add cherry tomatoes and drizzle with olive oil.
3. Sprinkle with black pepper and serve.

**Nutritional Information (Per Serving):**

- **Cal:** 340 kcal
- **Fat:** 12 g
- **Carbs:** 50 g
- **Proteins:** 10 g
- **Fiber:** 5 g

**Common Allergens:** Gluten (pasta), Nuts (pesto)

## 25. Chickpea & Avocado Toast

**Prep Time:** 5 minutes
**Cook Time:** 2 minutes
**Servings:** 1

**Ingredients:**

- 1 slice whole grain bread
- 1/2 cup canned chickpeas, mashed
- 1/2 avocado, mashed
- 1 teaspoon lemon juice
- 1/4 teaspoon black pepper

**Instructions:**

1. Toast the bread.
2. Mix mashed chickpeas, avocado, and lemon juice.
3. Spread onto the toast and sprinkle with black pepper.
4. Serve immediately.

**Nutritional Information (Per Serving):**

- **Cal:** 300 kcal
- **Fat:** 11 g
- **Carbs:** 40 g
- **Proteins:** 10 g
- **Fiber:** 8 g

**Common Allergens:** Gluten (bread)

## 26. Avocado & Cucumber Sushi Rolls

**Prep Time:** 10 minutes
**Cook Time:** 0 minutes
**Servings:** 2

**Ingredients:**

- 1 cup cooked sushi rice
- 1 sheet nori (seaweed)
- 1/2 avocado, sliced
- 1/2 cucumber, julienned
- 1 teaspoon soy sauce

**Instructions:**

1. Lay the nori sheet on a flat surface.
2. Spread sushi rice evenly over the sheet.
3. Arrange avocado and cucumber along one edge.
4. Roll tightly, slice into pieces, and serve with soy sauce.

**Nutritional Information (Per Serving):**

- **Cal:** 220 kcal
- **Fat:** 7 g
- **Carbs:** 35 g
- **Proteins:** 5 g
- **Fiber:** 4 g

**Common Allergens:** Soy (soy sauce), Gluten (if using regular soy sauce)

## 27. Tomato Basil Toast

**Prep Time:** 5 minutes
**Cook Time:** 2 minutes
**Servings:** 1

**Ingredients:**

- 1 slice whole grain bread
- 1/2 cup cherry tomatoes, halved
- 1 teaspoon olive oil
- 1 teaspoon balsamic vinegar
- 3 fresh basil leaves, chopped

**Instructions:**

1. Toast the bread until golden.
2. Top with cherry tomatoes and chopped basil.
3. Drizzle with olive oil and balsamic vinegar.
4. Serve immediately.

**Nutritional Information (Per Serving):**

- **Cal:** 190 kcal
- **Fat:** 6 g
- **Carbs:** 28 g
- **Proteins:** 5 g
- **Fiber:** 4 g

**Common Allergens:** Gluten (bread)

## 28. Spicy Lentil Wrap

**Prep Time:** 5 minutes
**Cook Time:** 0 minutes
**Servings:** 2

**Ingredients:**

- 2 whole wheat tortillas
- 1 cup cooked lentils
- 1/2 cup shredded lettuce
- 1 teaspoon hot sauce
- 1/4 teaspoon cumin

**Instructions:**

1. Spread lentils evenly over the tortillas.
2. Sprinkle with cumin and hot sauce.
3. Add shredded lettuce, roll up, and serve.

**Nutritional Information (Per Serving):**

- **Cal:** 280 kcal
- **Fat:** 4 g
- **Carbs:** 45 g
- **Proteins:** 12 g
- **Fiber:** 8 g

**Common Allergens:** Gluten (tortillas)

## 29. Cucumber & Avocado Salad

**Prep Time:** 5 minutes
**Cook Time:** 0 minutes
**Servings:** 2

**Ingredients:**

- 1 cucumber, sliced
- 1/2 avocado, diced
- 1 teaspoon olive oil
- 1 teaspoon lemon juice
- 1/4 teaspoon black pepper

**Instructions:**

1. In a bowl, combine cucumber and avocado.
2. Drizzle with olive oil and lemon juice.
3. Sprinkle with black pepper and toss.
4. Serve immediately.

**Nutritional Information (Per Serving):**

- **Cal:** 180 kcal
- **Fat:** 9 g
- **Carbs:** 20 g
- **Proteins:** 4 g
- **Fiber:** 5 g

**Common Allergens:** None

## 30. Roasted Chickpea Wrap

**Prep Time:** 5 minutes
**Cook Time:** 10 minutes
**Servings:** 2

**Ingredients:**

- 1 cup canned chickpeas, drained
- 1 teaspoon olive oil
- 1/2 teaspoon smoked paprika
- 2 whole wheat tortillas
- 1/2 cup shredded lettuce

**Instructions:**

1. Preheat oven to 400°F (200°C).
2. Toss chickpeas with olive oil and smoked paprika. Roast for 10 minutes.
3. Fill tortillas with roasted chickpeas and shredded lettuce.
4. Serve warm.

**Nutritional Information (Per Serving):**

- **Cal:** 290 kcal
- **Fat:** 7 g
- **Carbs:** 45 g
- **Proteins:** 10 g
- **Fiber:** 8 g

**Common Allergens:** Gluten (tortillas)

# DINNER RECIPES

## 1. Garlic Mushroom Quinoa

**Prep Time:** 5 minutes
**Cook Time:** 15 minutes
**Servings:** 2

**Ingredients:**

- 1 cup cooked quinoa
- 1 cup sliced mushrooms
- 2 cloves garlic, minced
- 1 teaspoon olive oil
- 1/2 teaspoon black pepper

**Instructions:**

1. Heat olive oil in a pan over medium heat.
2. Add garlic and sauté for 1 minute.
3. Stir in mushrooms and cook until tender.
4. Add quinoa and black pepper, mixing well.
5. Serve warm.

**Nutritional Information (Per Serving):**

- **Cal:** 230 kcal
- **Fat:** 6 g
- **Carbs:** 35 g
- **Proteins:** 8 g
- **Fiber:** 5 g

**Common Allergens:** None

## 2. Lentil Tomato Stew

**Prep Time:** 5 minutes
**Cook Time:** 20 minutes
**Servings:** 2

**Ingredients:**

- 1 cup cooked lentils
- 1 cup canned diced tomatoes
- 1/2 teaspoon cumin
- 1/2 teaspoon smoked paprika
- 1 teaspoon olive oil

**Instructions:**

1. Heat olive oil in a pot over medium heat.
2. Add cumin and smoked paprika, stirring for 30 seconds.
3. Stir in lentils and diced tomatoes.
4. Simmer for 10-15 minutes.
5. Serve warm.

**Nutritional Information (Per Serving):**

- **Cal:** 250 kcal
- **Fat:** 5 g
- **Carbs:** 40 g
- **Proteins:** 12 g
- **Fiber:** 8 g

**Common Allergens:** None

## 3. Chickpea Stir-Fry

**Prep Time:** 5 minutes
**Cook Time:** 10 minutes
**Servings:** 2

**Ingredients:**

- 1 cup canned chickpeas, drained
- 1/2 cup bell peppers, sliced
- 1/2 cup broccoli florets
- 1 teaspoon soy sauce
- 1 teaspoon olive oil

**Instructions:**

1. Heat olive oil in a pan over medium heat.
2. Add bell peppers and broccoli, sauté for 5 minutes.
3. Stir in chickpeas and soy sauce, cooking for another 5 minutes.
4. Serve warm.

**Nutritional Information (Per Serving):**

- **Cal:** 260 kcal
- **Fat:** 7 g
- **Carbs:** 38 g
- **Proteins:** 10 g
- **Fiber:** 9 g

**Common Allergens:** Soy (soy sauce), Gluten (if using regular soy sauce)

## 4. Sweet Potato & Black Bean Tacos

**Prep Time:** 10 minutes
**Cook Time:** 15 minutes
**Servings:** 2

**Ingredients:**

- 2 whole wheat tortillas
- 1 cup mashed sweet potatoes
- 1/2 cup black beans
- 1/2 teaspoon cumin
- 1 teaspoon lime juice

**Instructions:**

1. Warm tortillas in a dry pan over medium heat.
2. Spread mashed sweet potatoes onto tortillas.
3. Add black beans, cumin, and lime juice.
4. Serve immediately.

**Nutritional Information (Per Serving):**

- **Cal:** 300 kcal
- **Fat:** 4 g
- **Carbs:** 55 g
- **Proteins:** 10 g
- **Fiber:** 10 g

**Common Allergens:** Gluten (tortillas)

## 5. Avocado Pasta

**Prep Time:** 5 minutes
**Cook Time:** 10 minutes
**Servings:** 2

**Ingredients:**

- 2 cups cooked whole wheat pasta
- 1/2 avocado, mashed
- 1 teaspoon lemon juice
- 1/2 teaspoon garlic powder
- 1 teaspoon olive oil

**Instructions:**

1. In a bowl, mix mashed avocado, lemon juice, garlic powder, and olive oil.
2. Toss with cooked pasta until coated.
3. Serve immediately.

**Nutritional Information (Per Serving):**

- **Cal:** 340 kcal
- **Fat:** 12 g
- **Carbs:** 50 g
- **Proteins:** 9 g
- **Fiber:** 7 g

**Common Allergens:** Gluten (pasta)

## 6. Teriyaki Tofu Bowl

**Prep Time:** 5 minutes
**Cook Time:** 10 minutes
**Servings:** 2

**Ingredients:**

- 1 cup cooked rice
- 1/2 cup cubed tofu
- 1 teaspoon teriyaki sauce
- 1/2 cup steamed broccoli
- 1 teaspoon sesame seeds

**Instructions:**

1. Heat a pan over medium heat and cook tofu until golden.
2. Stir in teriyaki sauce and cook for 2 more minutes.
3. Serve over rice with steamed broccoli and sesame seeds.

**Nutritional Information (Per Serving):**

- **Cal:** 320 kcal
- **Fat:** 8 g
- **Carbs:** 50 g
- **Proteins:** 12 g
- **Fiber:** 5 g

**Common Allergens:** Soy (tofu, teriyaki sauce), Sesame

## 7. Quinoa & Roasted Veggie Bowl

**Prep Time:** 5 minutes
**Cook Time:** 15 minutes
**Servings:** 2

**Ingredients:**

- 1 cup cooked quinoa
- 1/2 cup roasted bell peppers
- 1/2 cup roasted zucchini
- 1 teaspoon olive oil
- 1 teaspoon balsamic vinegar

**Instructions:**

1. Toss roasted vegetables with olive oil and balsamic vinegar.
2. Serve over quinoa.

**Nutritional Information (Per Serving):**

- **Cal:** 250 kcal
- **Fat:** 6 g
- **Carbs:** 40 g
- **Proteins:** 9 g
- **Fiber:** 6 g

**Common Allergens:** None

## 8. Spaghetti Marinara

**Prep Time:** 5 minutes
**Cook Time:** 10 minutes
**Servings:** 2

**Ingredients:**

- 2 cups cooked whole wheat spaghetti
- 1 cup marinara sauce
- 1/2 teaspoon oregano
- 1/2 teaspoon garlic powder
- 1 teaspoon olive oil

**Instructions:**

1. Heat marinara sauce in a pot over medium heat.
2. Stir in oregano, garlic powder, and olive oil.
3. Toss with cooked spaghetti and serve.

**Nutritional Information (Per Serving):**

- **Cal:** 330 kcal
- **Fat:** 7 g
- **Carbs:** 55 g
- **Proteins:** 10 g
- **Fiber:** 8 g

**Common Allergens:** Gluten (pasta)

## 9. Black Bean & Rice Bowl

**Prep Time:** 5 minutes
**Cook Time:** 10 minutes
**Servings:** 2

**Ingredients:**

- 1 cup cooked rice
- 1/2 cup black beans
- 1 teaspoon lime juice
- 1/2 teaspoon cumin
- 1 teaspoon olive oil

**Instructions:**

1. Heat black beans in a pan with olive oil, cumin, and lime juice.
2. Serve over rice.

**Nutritional Information (Per Serving):**

- **Cal:** 280 kcal
- **Fat:** 5 g
- **Carbs:** 45 g
- **Proteins:** 9 g
- **Fiber:** 7 g

**Common Allergens:** None

## 10. Stuffed Bell Peppers

**Prep Time:** 5 minutes
**Cook Time:** 15 minutes
**Servings:** 2

**Ingredients:**

- 2 bell peppers, halved
- 1 cup cooked quinoa
- 1/2 cup black beans
- 1/2 teaspoon chili powder
- 1 teaspoon olive oil

**Instructions:**

1. Stuff bell peppers with quinoa, black beans, and chili powder.
2. Drizzle with olive oil and bake at 375°F for 15 minutes.

**Nutritional Information (Per Serving):**

- **Cal:** 260 kcal
- **Fat:** 6 g
- **Carbs:** 40 g
- **Proteins:** 9 g
- **Fiber:** 7 g

**Common Allergens:** None

## 11. Garlic Spinach Rice

**Prep Time:** 5 minutes
**Cook Time:** 10 minutes
**Servings:** 2

**Ingredients:**

- 1 cup cooked rice
- 1 cup fresh spinach
- 2 cloves garlic, minced
- 1 teaspoon olive oil
- 1/2 teaspoon black pepper

**Instructions:**

1. Heat olive oil in a pan over medium heat.
2. Add garlic and sauté for 1 minute.
3. Stir in spinach and cook until wilted.
4. Mix in rice and black pepper.
5. Serve warm.

**Nutritional Information (Per Serving):**

- **Cal:** 220 kcal
- **Fat:** 5 g
- **Carbs:** 40 g
- **Proteins:** 6 g
- **Fiber:** 4 g

**Common Allergens:** None

## 12. Cauliflower Chickpea Curry

**Prep Time:** 5 minutes
**Cook Time:** 15 minutes
**Servings:** 2

**Ingredients:**

- 1 cup cooked chickpeas
- 1 cup cauliflower florets
- 1 cup coconut milk
- 1 teaspoon curry powder
- 1 teaspoon olive oil

**Instructions:**

1. Heat olive oil in a pot over medium heat.
2. Add cauliflower and cook for 5 minutes.
3. Stir in chickpeas, coconut milk, and curry powder.
4. Simmer for 10 minutes.
5. Serve warm.

**Nutritional Information (Per Serving):**

- **Cal:** 280 kcal
- **Fat:** 12 g
- **Carbs:** 35 g
- **Proteins:** 8 g
- **Fiber:** 6 g

**Common Allergens:** Coconut

## 13. Avocado Chickpea Salad

**Prep Time:** 5 minutes
**Cook Time:** 0 minutes
**Servings:** 2

**Ingredients:**

- 1 cup canned chickpeas, drained
- 1/2 avocado, mashed
- 1 teaspoon lemon juice
- 1/2 teaspoon garlic powder
- 1 teaspoon olive oil

**Instructions:**

1. In a bowl, mash chickpeas and avocado together.
2. Add lemon juice, garlic powder, and olive oil.
3. Mix well and serve.

**Nutritional Information (Per Serving):**

- **Cal:** 260 kcal
- **Fat:** 10 g
- **Carbs:** 35 g
- **Proteins:** 9 g
- **Fiber:** 7 g

**Common Allergens:** None

## 14. Roasted Sweet Potato & Kale

**Prep Time:** 5 minutes
**Cook Time:** 15 minutes
**Servings:** 2

**Ingredients:**

- 1 cup diced sweet potatoes
- 1 cup kale, chopped
- 1 teaspoon olive oil
- 1/2 teaspoon paprika
- 1/2 teaspoon garlic powder

**Instructions:**

1. Preheat oven to 400°F.
2. Toss sweet potatoes with olive oil, paprika, and garlic powder.
3. Roast for 15 minutes.
4. Stir in kale and roast for 5 more minutes.
5. Serve warm.

**Nutritional Information (Per Serving):**

- **Cal:** 250 kcal
- **Fat:** 6 g
- **Carbs:** 40 g
- **Proteins:** 5 g
- **Fiber:** 8 g

**Common Allergens:** None

## 15. Zucchini Noodles with Pesto

**Prep Time:** 5 minutes
**Cook Time:** 5 minutes
**Servings:** 2

**Ingredients:**

- 2 medium zucchinis, spiralized
- 2 tablespoons pesto (vegan)
- 1 teaspoon olive oil
- 1 teaspoon lemon juice
- 1/2 teaspoon garlic powder

**Instructions:**

1. Heat olive oil in a pan over medium heat.
2. Add zucchini noodles and cook for 2 minutes.
3. Stir in pesto, lemon juice, and garlic powder.
4. Toss and serve warm.

**Nutritional Information (Per Serving):**

- **Cal:** 180 kcal
- **Fat:** 10 g
- **Carbs:** 15 g
- **Proteins:** 4 g
- **Fiber:** 3 g

**Common Allergens:** Nuts (if pesto contains nuts)

## 16. Vegan Chili

**Prep Time:** 5 minutes
**Cook Time:** 15 minutes
**Servings:** 2

**Ingredients:**

- 1 cup cooked black beans
- 1 cup canned diced tomatoes
- 1/2 cup corn
- 1 teaspoon chili powder
- 1 teaspoon olive oil

**Instructions:**

1. Heat olive oil in a pot over medium heat.
2. Add all ingredients and mix well.
3. Simmer for 15 minutes.
4. Serve warm.

**Nutritional Information (Per Serving):**

- **Cal:** 270 kcal
- **Fat:** 5 g
- **Carbs:** 45 g
- **Proteins:** 10 g
- **Fiber:** 8 g

**Common Allergens:** None

## 17. Roasted Brussels Sprouts & Quinoa

**Prep Time:** 5 minutes
**Cook Time:** 15 minutes
**Servings:** 2

**Ingredients:**

- 1 cup cooked quinoa
- 1 cup Brussels sprouts, halved
- 1 teaspoon olive oil
- 1/2 teaspoon black pepper
- 1 teaspoon lemon juice

**Instructions:**

1. Preheat oven to 400°F.
2. Toss Brussels sprouts with olive oil and black pepper.
3. Roast for 15 minutes.
4. Serve over quinoa with lemon juice.

**Nutritional Information (Per Serving):**

- **Cal:** 240 kcal
- **Fat:** 6 g
- **Carbs:** 35 g
- **Proteins:** 9 g
- **Fiber:** 6 g

**Common Allergens:** None

## 18. Tofu & Spinach Stir-Fry

**Prep Time:** 5 minutes
**Cook Time:** 10 minutes
**Servings:** 2

**Ingredients:**

- 1 cup cubed tofu
- 1 cup fresh spinach
- 1 teaspoon soy sauce
- 1 teaspoon olive oil
- 1/2 teaspoon garlic powder

**Instructions:**

1. Heat olive oil in a pan over medium heat.
2. Add tofu and cook until golden.
3. Stir in spinach, soy sauce, and garlic powder.
4. Cook for another 2 minutes and serve.

**Nutritional Information (Per Serving):**

- **Cal:** 280 kcal
- **Fat:** 10 g
- **Carbs:** 30 g
- **Proteins:** 12 g
- **Fiber:** 5 g

**Common Allergens:** Soy

### 19. Roasted Carrot & Lentil Bowl

**Prep Time:** 5 minutes
**Cook Time:** 15 minutes
**Servings:** 2

**Ingredients:**

- 1 cup cooked lentils
- 1 cup roasted carrots
- 1 teaspoon olive oil
- 1/2 teaspoon cumin
- 1 teaspoon lemon juice

**Instructions:**

1. Toss carrots with olive oil and cumin, roast at 400°F for 15 minutes.
2. Serve over lentils with lemon juice.

**Nutritional Information (Per Serving):**

- **Cal:** 260 kcal
- **Fat:** 5 g
- **Carbs:** 40 g
- **Proteins:** 10 g
- **Fiber:** 7 g

**Common Allergens:** None

## 20. Garlic Roasted Cauliflower & Lentils

**Prep Time:** 5 minutes
**Cook Time:** 15 minutes
**Servings:** 2

**Ingredients:**

- 1 cup cooked lentils
- 1 cup cauliflower florets
- 1 teaspoon olive oil
- 1/2 teaspoon garlic powder
- 1/2 teaspoon black pepper

**Instructions:**

1. Toss cauliflower with olive oil, garlic powder, and black pepper.
2. Roast at 400°F for 15 minutes until golden.
3. Serve over cooked lentils.

**Nutritional Information (Per Serving):**

- **Cal:** 240 kcal
- **Fat:** 5 g
- **Carbs:** 35 g
- **Proteins:** 12 g
- **Fiber:** 9 g

**Common Allergens:** None

## 21. Black Bean Tacos

**Prep Time:** 5 minutes
**Cook Time:** 5 minutes
**Servings:** 2

**Ingredients:**

- 4 small corn tortillas
- 1 cup canned black beans, drained
- 1/2 cup diced tomatoes
- 1 teaspoon cumin
- 1 teaspoon lime juice

**Instructions:**

1. Heat black beans in a pan over medium heat with cumin.
2. Warm tortillas on a dry pan for 1 minute per side.
3. Fill tortillas with beans and diced tomatoes.
4. Drizzle with lime juice and serve.

**Nutritional Information (Per Serving):**

- **Cal:** 280 kcal
- **Fat:** 3 g
- **Carbs:** 50 g
- **Proteins:** 10 g
- **Fiber:** 9 g

**Common Allergens:** None

## 22. Sweet Potato & Black Bean Bowl

**Prep Time:** 5 minutes
**Cook Time:** 15 minutes
**Servings:** 2

**Ingredients:**

- 1 cup diced sweet potatoes
- 1 cup canned black beans, drained
- 1/2 teaspoon smoked paprika
- 1 teaspoon olive oil
- 1 teaspoon lime juice

**Instructions:**

1. Roast sweet potatoes at 400°F for 15 minutes.
2. Heat black beans in a pan with paprika.
3. Serve together with a drizzle of lime juice.

**Nutritional Information (Per Serving):**

- **Cal:** 270 kcal
- **Fat:** 5 g
- **Carbs:** 45 g
- **Proteins:** 9 g
- **Fiber:** 8 g

**Common Allergens:** None

## 23. Chickpea & Spinach Wrap

**Prep Time:** 5 minutes
**Cook Time:** 0 minutes
**Servings:** 2

**Ingredients:**

- 2 whole wheat tortillas
- 1 cup canned chickpeas, drained
- 1 cup fresh spinach
- 1 teaspoon tahini
- 1 teaspoon lemon juice

**Instructions:**

1. Mash chickpeas with tahini and lemon juice.
2. Spread mixture onto tortillas.
3. Add fresh spinach and roll up.
4. Serve immediately.

**Nutritional Information (Per Serving):**

- **Cal:** 320 kcal
- **Fat:** 7 g
- **Carbs:** 50 g
- **Proteins:** 12 g
- **Fiber:** 9 g

**Common Allergens:** Gluten (if using wheat tortillas), Sesame (tahini)

## 24. Tomato & Basil Pasta

**Prep Time:** 5 minutes
**Cook Time:** 10 minutes
**Servings:** 2

**Ingredients:**

- 2 cups cooked pasta
- 1 cup cherry tomatoes, halved
- 1 teaspoon olive oil
- 1 teaspoon minced garlic
- 5 fresh basil leaves

**Instructions:**

1. Heat olive oil in a pan over medium heat.
2. Sauté garlic for 1 minute, then add cherry tomatoes.
3. Cook for 5 minutes until soft.
4. Toss with pasta and fresh basil.
5. Serve warm.

**Nutritional Information (Per Serving):**

- **Cal:** 340 kcal
- **Fat:** 6 g
- **Carbs:** 60 g
- **Proteins:** 10 g
- **Fiber:** 5 g

**Common Allergens:** Gluten (if using regular pasta)

## 25. Lentil & Tomato Soup

**Prep Time:** 5 minutes
**Cook Time:** 15 minutes
**Servings:** 2

**Ingredients:**

- 1 cup cooked lentils
- 1 cup canned diced tomatoes
- 1 cup vegetable broth
- 1/2 teaspoon cumin
- 1 teaspoon olive oil

**Instructions:**

1. Heat olive oil in a pot over medium heat.
2. Add all ingredients and bring to a boil.
3. Simmer for 15 minutes.
4. Serve warm.

**Nutritional Information (Per Serving):**

- **Cal:** 250 kcal
- **Fat:** 5 g
- **Carbs:** 35 g
- **Proteins:** 12 g
- **Fiber:** 7 g

**Common Allergens:** None

## 26. Roasted Broccoli & Quinoa Bowl

**Prep Time:** 5 minutes
**Cook Time:** 15 minutes
**Servings:** 2

**Ingredients:**

- 1 cup cooked quinoa
- 1 cup broccoli florets
- 1 teaspoon olive oil
- 1/2 teaspoon garlic powder
- 1 teaspoon lemon juice

**Instructions:**

1. Toss broccoli with olive oil and garlic powder.
2. Roast at 400°F for 15 minutes.
3. Serve over quinoa with lemon juice.

**Nutritional Information (Per Serving):**

- **Cal:** 240 kcal
- **Fat:** 6 g
- **Carbs:** 35 g
- **Proteins:** 8 g
- **Fiber:** 6 g

**Common Allergens:** None

## 27. Sautéed Mushrooms & Brown Rice

**Prep Time:** 5 minutes
**Cook Time:** 10 minutes
**Servings:** 2

**Ingredients:**

- 1 cup cooked brown rice
- 1 cup sliced mushrooms
- 1 teaspoon olive oil
- 1/2 teaspoon soy sauce
- 1/2 teaspoon garlic powder

**Instructions:**

1. Heat olive oil in a pan over medium heat.
2. Add mushrooms, soy sauce, and garlic powder.
3. Cook for 5 minutes until soft.
4. Serve over brown rice.

**Nutritional Information (Per Serving):**

- **Cal:** 260 kcal
- **Fat:** 5 g
- **Carbs:** 45 g
- **Proteins:** 7 g
- **Fiber:** 5 g

**Common Allergens:** Soy (if using soy sauce)

## 28. Spicy Peanut Noodles

**Prep Time:** 5 minutes
**Cook Time:** 10 minutes
**Servings:** 2

**Ingredients:**

- 2 cups cooked rice noodles
- 1 tablespoon peanut butter
- 1 teaspoon soy sauce
- 1 teaspoon sriracha
- 1 teaspoon lime juice

**Instructions:**

1. Whisk peanut butter, soy sauce, sriracha, and lime juice together.
2. Toss with cooked rice noodles.
3. Serve immediately.

**Nutritional Information (Per Serving):**

- **Cal:** 320 kcal
- **Fat:** 9 g
- **Carbs:** 55 g
- **Proteins:** 10 g
- **Fiber:** 4 g

**Common Allergens:** Nuts (peanut butter), Soy (soy sauce)

## 29. Roasted Chickpeas & Veggies

**Prep Time:** 5 minutes
**Cook Time:** 15 minutes
**Servings:** 2

**Ingredients:**

- 1 cup canned chickpeas, drained
- 1 cup mixed vegetables (zucchini, bell pepper, onion)
- 1 teaspoon olive oil
- 1/2 teaspoon paprika
- 1/2 teaspoon salt

**Instructions:**

1. Toss all ingredients together.
2. Roast at 400°F for 15 minutes.
3. Serve warm.

**Nutritional Information (Per Serving):**

- **Cal:** 250 kcal
- **Fat:** 6 g
- **Carbs:** 35 g
- **Proteins:** 9 g
- **Fiber:** 6 g

**Common Allergens:** None

## 30. Quinoa & Avocado Bowl

**Prep Time:** 5 minutes
**Cook Time:** 0 minutes
**Servings:** 2

**Ingredients:**

- 1 cup cooked quinoa
- 1/2 avocado, diced
- 1 teaspoon lemon juice
- 1 teaspoon olive oil
- 1/2 teaspoon black pepper

**Instructions:**

1. Toss all ingredients together in a bowl.
2. Serve immediately.

**Nutritional Information (Per Serving):**

- **Cal:** 280 kcal
- **Fat:** 10 g
- **Carbs:** 40 g
- **Proteins:** 9 g
- **Fiber:** 7 g

**Common Allergens:** None

# SNACK RECIPES

## 1. Almond Butter Apple Slices

**Prep Time:** 3 minutes
**Cook Time:** 0 minutes
**Servings:** 1

**Ingredients:**

- 1 apple, sliced
- 1 tablespoon almond butter
- 1 teaspoon chia seeds
- 1 teaspoon cinnamon
- 1 teaspoon maple syrup

**Instructions:**

1. Arrange apple slices on a plate.
2. Drizzle almond butter over the slices.
3. Sprinkle chia seeds and cinnamon on top.
4. Drizzle with maple syrup and serve.

**Nutritional Information (Per Serving):**

- **Cal:** 220 kcal
- **Fat:** 9 g
- **Carbs:** 35 g
- **Proteins:** 3 g
- **Fiber:** 6 g

**Common Allergens:** Nuts (Almond Butter)

## 2. Avocado Rice Cakes

**Prep Time:** 3 minutes
**Cook Time:** 0 minutes
**Servings:** 1

**Ingredients:**

- 1 rice cake
- 1/2 avocado, mashed
- 1 teaspoon lemon juice
- 1/2 teaspoon black pepper
- Pinch of salt

**Instructions:**

1. Spread mashed avocado on the rice cake.
2. Drizzle with lemon juice.
3. Sprinkle with black pepper and salt.
4. Serve immediately.

**Nutritional Information (Per Serving):**

- **Cal:** 180 kcal
- **Fat:** 10 g
- **Carbs:** 20 g
- **Proteins:** 3 g
- **Fiber:** 5 g

**Common Allergens:** None

## 3. Banana Peanut Butter Bites

**Prep Time:** 2 minutes
**Cook Time:** 0 minutes
**Servings:** 1

**Ingredients:**

- 1 banana, sliced
- 1 tablespoon peanut butter
- 1 teaspoon chia seeds
- 1 teaspoon cocoa powder
- 1 teaspoon maple syrup

**Instructions:**

1. Spread peanut butter on half of the banana slices.
2. Top with remaining banana slices to make mini sandwiches.
3. Sprinkle with chia seeds and cocoa powder.
4. Drizzle with maple syrup and serve.

**Nutritional Information (Per Serving):**

- **Cal:** 250 kcal
- **Fat:** 10 g
- **Carbs:** 35 g
- **Proteins:** 5 g
- **Fiber:** 6 g

**Common Allergens:** Nuts (Peanut Butter)

## 4. Hummus & Cucumber Bites

**Prep Time:** 3 minutes
**Cook Time:** 0 minutes
**Servings:** 1

**Ingredients:**

- 1/2 cucumber, sliced
- 2 tablespoons hummus
- 1 teaspoon sesame seeds
- 1 teaspoon lemon juice
- 1/2 teaspoon black pepper

**Instructions:**

1. Arrange cucumber slices on a plate.
2. Spread hummus on each slice.
3. Sprinkle with sesame seeds and black pepper.
4. Drizzle with lemon juice and serve.

**Nutritional Information (Per Serving):**

- **Cal:** 180 kcal
- **Fat:** 7 g
- **Carbs:** 18 g
- **Proteins:** 6 g
- **Fiber:** 5 g

**Common Allergens:** Sesame

## 5. Roasted Chickpeas

**Prep Time:** 5 minutes
**Cook Time:** 15 minutes
**Servings:** 2

**Ingredients:**

- 1 cup cooked chickpeas
- 1 teaspoon olive oil
- 1 teaspoon paprika
- 1/2 teaspoon salt
- 1/2 teaspoon black pepper

**Instructions:**

1. Toss chickpeas with olive oil, paprika, salt, and black pepper.
2. Roast at 400°F for 15 minutes until crispy.
3. Let cool slightly and serve.

**Nutritional Information (Per Serving):**

- **Cal:** 210 kcal
- **Fat:** 6 g
- **Carbs:** 30 g
- **Proteins:** 8 g
- **Fiber:** 7 g

**Common Allergens:** None

## 6. Dark Chocolate Almond Clusters

**Prep Time:** 5 minutes
**Cook Time:** 0 minutes
**Servings:** 2

**Ingredients:**

- 1/2 cup almonds
- 1/4 cup dark chocolate chips (vegan)
- 1 teaspoon coconut oil
- 1 teaspoon maple syrup
- 1/2 teaspoon sea salt

**Instructions:**

1. Melt dark chocolate chips with coconut oil in a microwave-safe bowl, stirring every 20 seconds until smooth.
2. Stir in almonds and mix until coated.
3. Drop spoonfuls onto parchment paper and sprinkle with sea salt.
4. Let set in the fridge for 20 minutes before serving.

**Nutritional Information (Per Serving):**

- **Cal:** 240 kcal
- **Fat:** 16 g
- **Carbs:** 20 g
- **Proteins:** 5 g
- **Fiber:** 4 g

**Common Allergens:** Nuts (Almonds)

## 7. Peanut Butter Oat Balls

**Prep Time:** 5 minutes
**Cook Time:** 0 minutes
**Servings:** 2

**Ingredients:**

- 1/2 cup rolled oats
- 2 tablespoons peanut butter
- 1 tablespoon maple syrup
- 1 teaspoon chia seeds
- 1 teaspoon cocoa powder

**Instructions:**

1. In a bowl, mix all ingredients until well combined.
2. Roll into small balls.
3. Refrigerate for 10 minutes before serving.

**Nutritional Information (Per Serving):**

- **Cal:** 210 kcal
- **Fat:** 10 g
- **Carbs:** 26 g
- **Proteins:** 5 g
- **Fiber:** 4 g

**Common Allergens:** Nuts (Peanut Butter), Gluten (if using non-certified gluten-free oats)

## 8. Stuffed Dates

**Prep Time:** 3 minutes
**Cook Time:** 0 minutes
**Servings:** 2

**Ingredients:**

- 6 Medjool dates, pitted
- 2 tablespoons almond butter
- 1 teaspoon shredded coconut
- 1 teaspoon cinnamon
- 1 teaspoon chopped walnuts

**Instructions:**

1. Slice each date open and fill with almond butter.
2. Sprinkle shredded coconut, cinnamon, and walnuts on top.
3. Serve immediately.

**Nutritional Information (Per Serving):**

- **Cal:** 250 kcal
- **Fat:** 10 g
- **Carbs:** 35 g
- **Proteins:** 4 g
- **Fiber:** 5 g

**Common Allergens:** Nuts (Almond Butter, Walnuts)

## 9. Veggie Wraps

**Prep Time:** 5 minutes
**Cook Time:** 0 minutes
**Servings:** 1

**Ingredients:**

- 1 whole wheat tortilla
- 1/4 avocado, mashed
- 1/4 cup shredded carrots
- 1/4 cup cucumber slices
- 1 teaspoon hummus

**Instructions:**

1. Spread mashed avocado and hummus on the tortilla.
2. Add shredded carrots and cucumber slices.
3. Roll tightly, slice in half, and serve.

**Nutritional Information (Per Serving):**

- **Cal:** 230 kcal
- **Fat:** 9 g
- **Carbs:** 32 g
- **Proteins:** 6 g
- **Fiber:** 6 g

**Common Allergens:** Gluten (if using regular tortilla)

## 10. Baked Sweet Potato Chips

**Prep Time:** 5 minutes
**Cook Time:** 15 minutes
**Servings:** 2

**Ingredients:**

- 1 large sweet potato, thinly sliced
- 1 teaspoon olive oil
- 1/2 teaspoon salt
- 1/2 teaspoon paprika
- 1/2 teaspoon black pepper

**Instructions:**

1. Toss sweet potato slices with olive oil, salt, paprika, and black pepper.
2. Arrange on a baking sheet and bake at 375°F for 15 minutes, flipping halfway.
3. Let cool and serve.

**Nutritional Information (Per Serving):**

- **Cal:** 180 kcal
- **Fat:** 4 g
- **Carbs:** 32 g
- **Proteins:** 2 g
- **Fiber:** 5 g

**Common Allergens:** None

## 11. Cucumber & Hummus Roll-Ups

**Prep Time:** 5 minutes
**Cook Time:** 0 minutes
**Servings:** 1

**Ingredients:**

- 1 cucumber, thinly sliced lengthwise
- 2 tablespoons hummus
- 1 teaspoon sesame seeds
- 1 teaspoon lemon juice
- Pinch of black pepper

**Instructions:**

1. Spread hummus onto each cucumber slice.
2. Roll up and secure with a toothpick if needed.
3. Sprinkle with sesame seeds, lemon juice, and black pepper.
4. Serve immediately.

**Nutritional Information (Per Serving):**

- **Cal:** 150 kcal
- **Fat:** 6 g
- **Carbs:** 18 g
- **Proteins:** 5 g
- **Fiber:** 4 g

**Common Allergens:** Sesame

## 12. Coconut Date Energy Bites

**Prep Time:** 5 minutes
**Cook Time:** 0 minutes
**Servings:** 2

**Ingredients:**

- 6 Medjool dates, pitted
- 1/4 cup shredded coconut
- 1 tablespoon almond butter
- 1 teaspoon cocoa powder
- 1 teaspoon chia seeds

**Instructions:**

1. Blend all ingredients in a food processor until well combined.
2. Roll into small balls.
3. Refrigerate for 10 minutes before serving.

**Nutritional Information (Per Serving):**

- **Cal:** 260 kcal
- **Fat:** 12 g
- **Carbs:** 35 g
- **Proteins:** 5 g
- **Fiber:** 6 g

**Common Allergens:** Nuts (Almond Butter)

## 13. Chocolate-Dipped Strawberries

**Prep Time:** 5 minutes
**Cook Time:** 0 minutes
**Servings:** 2

**Ingredients:**

- 6 strawberries
- 1/4 cup dark chocolate chips (vegan)
- 1 teaspoon coconut oil
- 1 teaspoon chopped almonds
- 1 teaspoon shredded coconut

**Instructions:**

1. Melt dark chocolate chips with coconut oil.
2. Dip each strawberry into the melted chocolate.
3. Sprinkle with chopped almonds and shredded coconut.
4. Let set in the fridge for 10 minutes before serving.

**Nutritional Information (Per Serving):**

- **Cal:** 180 kcal
- **Fat:** 9 g
- **Carbs:** 25 g
- **Proteins:** 3 g
- **Fiber:** 4 g

**Common Allergens:** Nuts (Almonds)

## 14. Guacamole & Crackers

**Prep Time:** 5 minutes
**Cook Time:** 0 minutes
**Servings:** 2

**Ingredients:**

- 1 avocado, mashed
- 1/2 teaspoon garlic powder
- 1 teaspoon lime juice
- 1/2 teaspoon salt
- 6 whole-grain crackers

**Instructions:**

1. Mix mashed avocado with garlic powder, lime juice, and salt.
2. Serve with whole-grain crackers.

**Nutritional Information (Per Serving):**

- **Cal:** 200 kcal
- **Fat:** 12 g
- **Carbs:** 22 g
- **Proteins:** 4 g
- **Fiber:** 6 g

**Common Allergens:** Gluten (if using non-gluten-free crackers)

## 15. Roasted Chickpeas

**Prep Time:** 5 minutes
**Cook Time:** 20 minutes
**Servings:** 2

**Ingredients:**

- 1 cup canned chickpeas, drained and rinsed
- 1 teaspoon olive oil
- 1/2 teaspoon paprika
- 1/2 teaspoon garlic powder
- 1/2 teaspoon salt

**Instructions:**

1. Preheat oven to 400°F.
2. Pat chickpeas dry with a paper towel.
3. Toss chickpeas with olive oil, paprika, garlic powder, and salt.
4. Spread evenly on a baking sheet and bake for 20 minutes, shaking halfway through.
5. Let cool slightly and serve.

**Nutritional Information (Per Serving):**

- **Cal:** 180 kcal
- **Fat:** 5 g
- **Carbs:** 26 g
- **Proteins:** 7 g
- **Fiber:** 6 g

**Common Allergens:** None

**ENJOY YOUR MEALS**

Made in United States
Troutdale, OR
03/06/2025